Animals in Winter

Animals in Winter

Vanessa Luff

Adam & Charles Black · London

In the autumn, some animals store food for the winter months ahead. Squirrels and jays bury nuts to eat when food is difficult to find.

Many animals sleep through the winter. This is called hibernation. The hedgehog lines a hole with moss and dry leaves, curling up from October until late March.

The dormouse does not sleep right through the winter. Sometimes it wakes, and feeds on nuts which it stored in the autumn.

Reptiles and amphibians hibernate too. They hide in holes and cracks during the cold months. Crested newts often spend the winter together, wound up in tight balls. The adder may curl up in an old bird's nest.

Animals can keep warm by huddling together. Wrens and ladybirds are very different creatures, but they both huddle together for the winter.

Many rare birds are forced out into the open to look for food. These are waxwings, feeding from a crop of bright red berries.

If you put out food for birds, you may attract many kinds seldom seen in gardens. Some are visitors from colder countries.

Shortage of food can force shy deer out of the woods—into your garden vegetable patch!

The stoat is a hunter. In winter, its coat of brown turns to white. In the snow, the stoat can surprise its prey.

The ptarmigan also turns white in winter. Its white plumage helps hide it from its enemies.

Hunger changes habits. Birds which normally feed alone will join flocks, to increase their chances of finding food.

The warmth of a house attracts a variety of wildlife. Insects, and perhaps a long-tailed field mouse, come in to escape the cold winter weather.

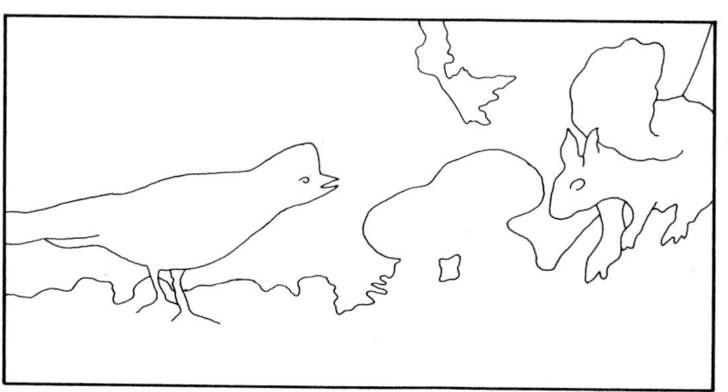

Food is plentiful in the autumn, and animals take advantage of the glut to see them through the winter. An enormous amount of food is consumed, laying down valuable fat as an insulating layer, and as a reserve for the coming time of near starvation. Many creatures collect and store nuts and seeds, returning to eat them during winter when other food is difficult to find.

A red squirrel and a jay are quarrelling over the acorns of the turkey oak as both make caches of nuts and acorns. The boletus fungus will be eaten now, since it won't keep in store.

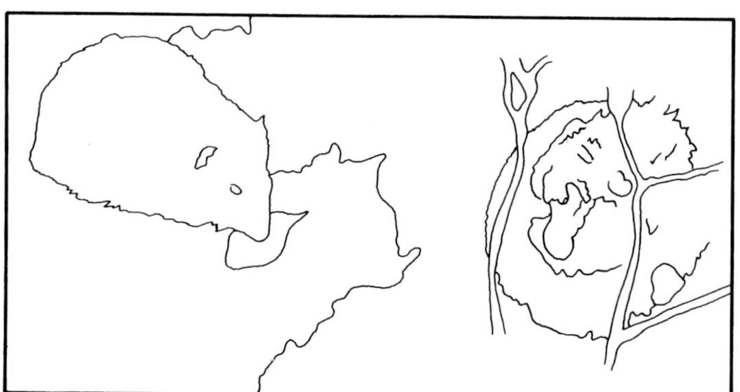

Hibernation is a very efficient way of passing the winter. Deep sleep slows down the metabolism. With very low energy demands, the animal can exist on stored fat alone.

The winter quarters of the hedgehog can be a hole under the roots of a tree, lined with leaves and moss. The hedgehog will sleep curled up in this 'hibernaculum' from October until the end of March. During this time its body temperature drops and its pulse and breathing are hardly detectable. Extremes of cold will arouse the hedgehog, which will then find somewhere more sheltered to spend the remainder of the winter.

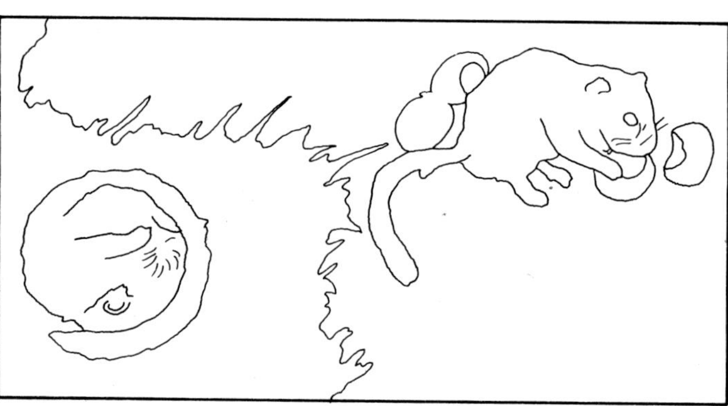

If a hibernating dormouse is accidentally spilt from its nest, it remains in a rigid ball with its tail curled up over its head. It is cold to the touch and shows all the appearances of death. Its winter sleep is not as continuous as that of the hedgehog: it wakes at intervals and feeds off a store of nuts gathered in the autumn. It then returns to its hibernaculum and resumes its curled up position, sleeping as deeply as before.

Cold blooded animals have to hibernate. They become progressively more sluggish as their temperature drops and have to shelter to avoid being frozen solid. An adder will find a dry hole or an old bird's nest low in the bushes, where it will coil up during the coldest months. As the weather warms up, the snake moves to a sunny bank to absorb heat and once more bring its body back to peak performance.

Amphibians often spend the winter deep in the mud at the bottom of the pond. Others, such as the great crested newt, come out of the water and congregate in damp holes, twisting together in a ball to avoid dehydration.

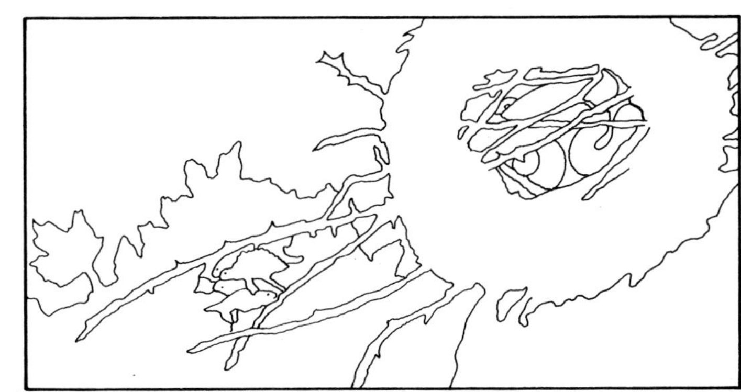

A collection of small creatures overwintering together is a common sight. Many insects do not survive the winter at all, but some are found in groups, hiding in fairly moist places—such as these ladybirds behind a curtain of foliage in an old wall.

More exciting is a huddle of wrens. Up to a dozen have been found desperately trying to keep warm in the shelter of old nest boxes, holes in walls or even coconut shells.

Very few birds hibernate; most species remain active throughout the year, migrating to avoid the worst of the cold weather and to find sufficient food. Some of the common summer birds fly to warmer climates, and birds from colder countries take their place.

The waxwing is a rare occasional visitor rather than a true migrant, but a large influx, or "waxwing winter" could bring them into suburban gardens. A party of waxwings can strip a shrub of berries in a very short time; one waxwing can consume more than its own weight in less than three hours.

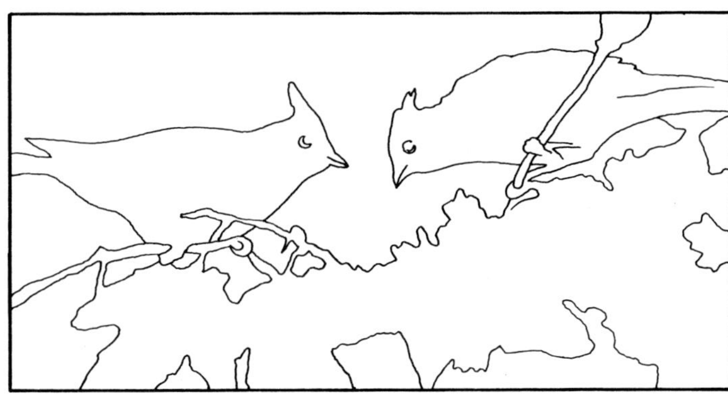

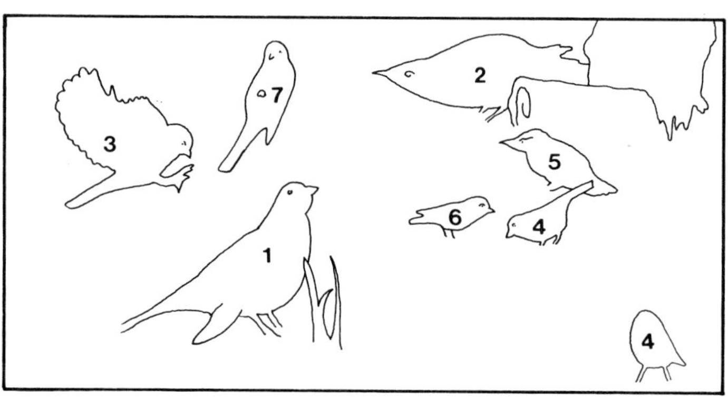

True winter migrants to Britain and Ireland include redwings (1) and fieldfares (2), both members of the thrush family from Scandinavia. Although these are field birds they can be enticed into gardens with wild bird food which they might share with other common garden birds such as the robin (3) and coal tits (4). Others from the surrounding countryside overcome their shyness in their search for food. These include the nuthatch (5), goldcrest (6) and linnet (7).

Snowdrops are one of the earliest plants to flower, often emerging through the covering of snow.

A large mammal like the deer can suffer badly from cold and starvation. Deciduous leaves, which form a large part of their diet, have all fallen and ground plants such as clover, heather and small shrubs can be under a thick layer of snow. These conditions will force the shy roe deer to venture near houses and to raid garden vegetables, leaving chewed stumps of brussels sprouts and their tracks or slots as evidence of the visit.

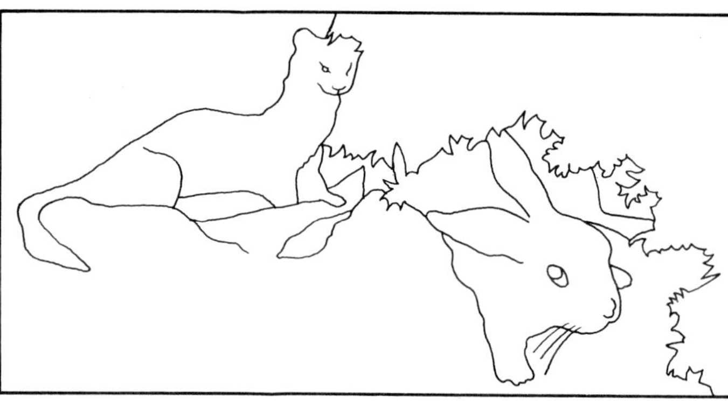

The change in the colour of the winter landscape, from warm browns and greens to greybrowns and whites makes some creatures, which are normally well camouflaged, very obvious. Some animals have overcome this problem by changing their colour when they grow their thick winter coats.

In Scotland and northern Europe, where winter snows are normal, the stoat loses its reddish brown coat and gains one of pure white, except for the tip of its tail. In this state it is known as an ermine.

The white hairs grow under the brown so that when the temperature drops and day length lessens the brown hairs are shed revealing the white beneath.

Cold blooded animals have to hibernate. They become progressively more sluggish as their temperature drops and have to shelter to avoid being frozen solid. An adder will find a dry hole or an old bird's nest low in the bushes, where it will coil up during the coldest months. As the weather warms up, the snake moves to a sunny bank to absorb heat and once more bring its body back to peak performance.

Amphibians often spend the winter deep in the mud at the bottom of the pond. Others, such as the great crested newt, come out of the water and congregate in damp holes, twisting together in a ball to avoid dehydration.

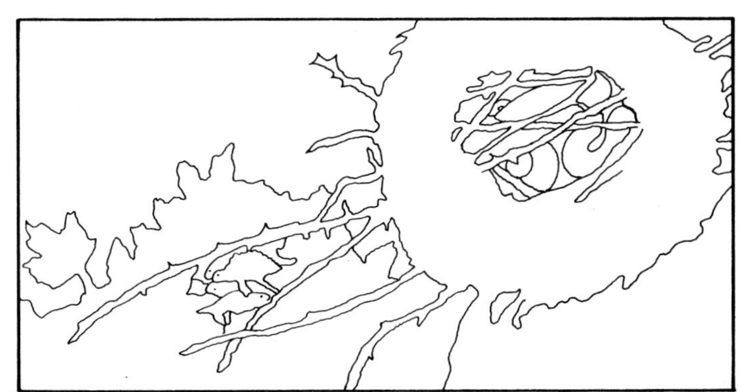

A collection of small creatures overwintering together is a common sight. Many insects do not survive the winter at all, but some are found in groups, hiding in fairly moist places—such as these ladybirds behind a curtain of foliage in an old wall.

More exciting is a huddle of wrens. Up to a dozen have been found desperately trying to keep warm in the shelter of old nest boxes, holes in walls or even coconut shells.

Very few birds hibernate; most species remain active throughout the year, migrating to avoid the worst of the cold weather and to find sufficient food. Some of the common summer birds fly to warmer climates, and birds from colder countries take their place.

The waxwing is a rare occasional visitor rather than a true migrant, but a large influx, or "waxwing winter" could bring them into suburban gardens. A party of waxwings can strip a shrub of berries in a very short time; one waxwing can consume more than its own weight in less than three hours.

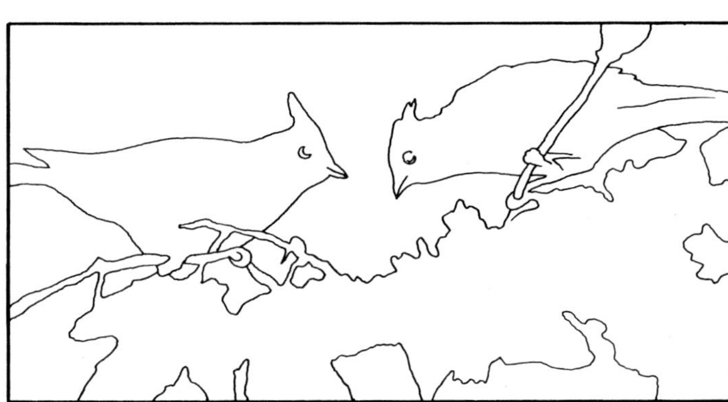

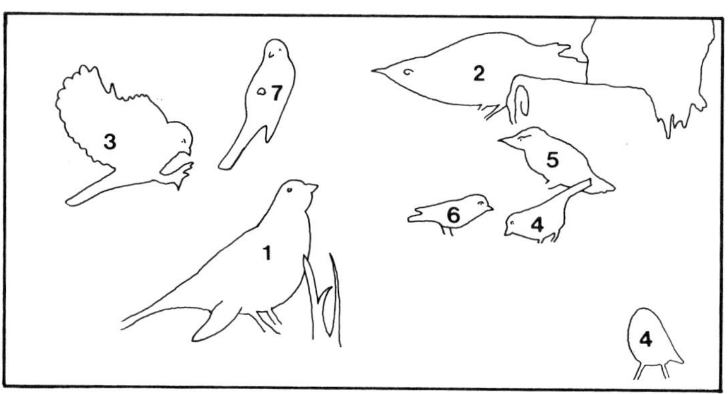

True winter migrants to Britain and Ireland include redwings (1) and fieldfares (2), both members of the thrush family from Scandinavia. Although these are field birds they can be enticed into gardens with wild bird food which they might share with other common garden birds such as the robin (3) and coal tits (4). Others from the surrounding countryside overcome their shyness in their search for food. These include the nuthatch (5), goldcrest (6) and linnet (7).

Snowdrops are one of the earliest plants to flower, often emerging through the covering of snow.

A large mammal like the deer can suffer badly from cold and starvation. Deciduous leaves, which form a large part of their diet, have all fallen and ground plants such as clover, heather and small shrubs can be under a thick layer of snow. These conditions will force the shy roe deer to venture near houses and to raid garden vegetables, leaving chewed stumps of brussels sprouts and their tracks or slots as evidence of the visit.

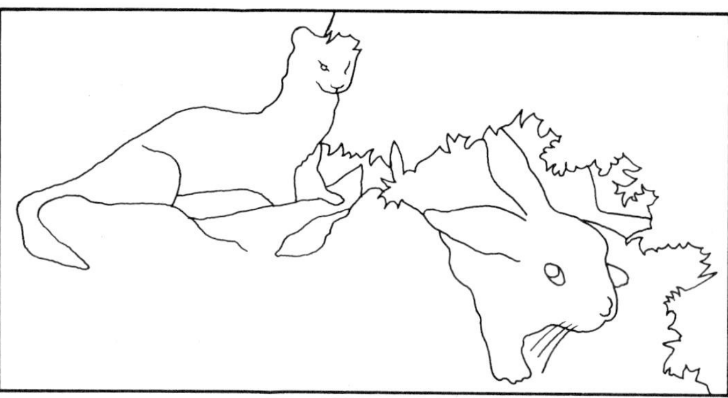

The change in the colour of the winter landscape, from warm browns and greens to greybrowns and whites makes some creatures, which are normally well camouflaged, very obvious. Some animals have overcome this problem by changing their colour when they grow their thick winter coats.

In Scotland and northern Europe, where winter snows are normal, the stoat loses its reddish brown coat and gains one of pure white, except for the tip of its tail. In this state it is known as an ermine.

The white hairs grow under the brown so that when the temperature drops and day length lessens the brown hairs are shed revealing the white beneath.

Camouflage is even more vital for a bird that is hunted. The ptarmigan is a mountain bird living in Scotland and northern Europe. It changes colour slowly with the seasons. In summer only its chest and wings are white and they are well hidden as the bird crouches in the heather and bilberries; its brown and black mottled back merge with the vegetation. As autumn progresses, the brown feathers are gradually replaced with white, giving the bird a blotchy grey appearance. By the time the snow arrives, the bird is completely white except for a black tail, red wattle and dark eye stripe.

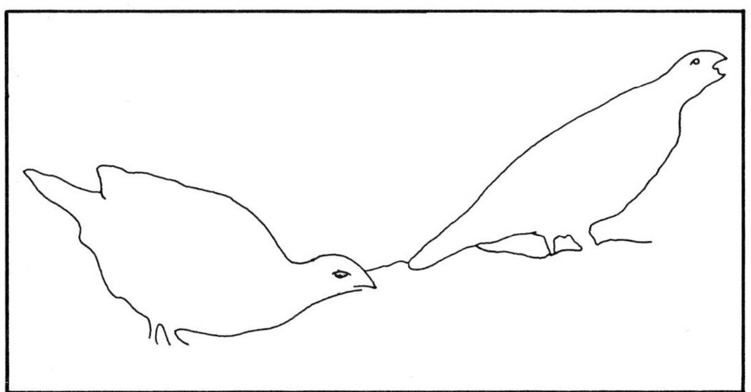

Foraging flocks of birds are a common sight in country hedgerows in winter. Birds which normally feed alone become gregarious, gathering with other species of seed eaters to gain a better chance of finding any remaining food.

A mixed flock could consist of goldfinches (1), redpolls (2), siskins (3), bullfinches (4), bramblings (5), greenfinches (6), yellowhammers (7), tree sparrows (8) and chaffinches (9).

Some animals and insects will come into buildings to shelter from the cold and may even venture into the house. A long tailed field mouse can sometimes be seen indoors, but it will not share winter quarters with the house mouse.

Insects may hide behind curtains, the corners of windows or the backs of shelves. House flies, lacewings and small tortoiseshell butterflies are commonly found.

They are often unnoticed during the winter, and are only seen in the spring when they try to find their way out again.

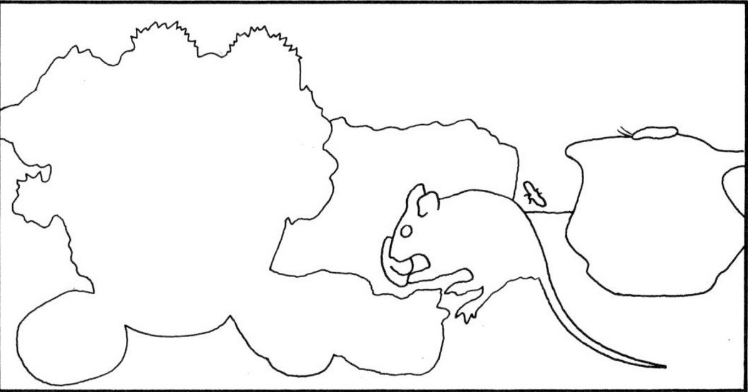

Published by A & C Black (Publishers) Ltd
35 Bedford Row, London WC1R 4JH

ISBN 0 7136 2009 9

First published 1979

Printed in Great Britain by W S Cowell Ltd, Ipswich